COMET DREAMS

LINDA KELLER

for J. E. Keller

North Carolina Hillbilly

1916 — 2000

ACKNOWLEDGMENTS

"Not Right" first appeared in *Mad Blood*, Issue #2, October, 2003.

"Open" first appeared in *Mad Blood*, Issue #2, October, 2003.

"What a Poem Can Be" first appeared in *Through All Your Blue Thoughts*, April, 2004, Littleton Public Schools.

Copyright 2004 by Linda Keller

All rights reserved. Printed in the United States of America. No part of this book may be used or reproduced in any manner whatsoever without written permission except in the case of brief quotations embodied in critical articles and reviews. For information address Tindari Press, 1035 South Ogden Street, Denver, Colorado 80209

First Edition

Graphic design, cover and illustrations by John Boak

Library of Congress Control Number: 2004095124

ISBN#0-9625718-3-0

Contents

Not Right	1
Linda, The Sculpture	2
Open	4
Perfect Afternoon	5
Stream, St. Louis Lake Trail	7
The Woodpecker Arrives	8
I am in the Water Poem	9
How Long Can I Stay Here?	11
Wishes	12
September 11, 2001	15
Winter Morning	16
Without Introduction	17
Outdoor Orchestra	19
Vendor	20
Rusted Key	21
What You Have Become	22
Inside	23
Current Creek	25
North Carolina Hillbilly	26
Summer of Fires	29
Leonid Meteor Shower	30
High Cholesterol Blues	31
To Be Deaf	33
Seed of Joy	34
Snatches of Space	35
Backwards	36
Funeral	39
When She Smiles	40
Bitter	42
Laid Off	43
For Chuck on his 80th Birthday	44
Julia	45
Aunt Lala	46
Lost	48
Can You See?	49
Prison	51
Hiking Questions in Canyonlands	53
The Visitor	54
Eye to Eye	55
Eddy	57
The Details	58
What a Poem Can Be	61
Index of Illustrations	63
About the Author & the Artist	65

NOT RIGHT

Feet clump against
the wooden planks
of the boardwalk,
transport me to the Jersey shore.
I'm thirteen years old.
Hair won't stay straight in the humidity
though I've ironed it and wrapped it around
a coffee can for two hours.
I've got my pink, dotted swiss
triangle scarf on.
We wander into the arcades of Mannasquan,
look down as we walk past
the boys.
Red lights pulse, music blares,
occasionally a prize is won.
Somehow I wind up with a six foot long
lime green snake,
but no dates.
Why can't my hair be straight?
I roll my pale yellow pedal pushers
up one notch higher,
my legs brown as wet sand.
Back out on the boardwalk
the moist, salty breeze
lifts my hair
into a clownish frizz.
Even the scarf won't keep it down.

God I'm glad I'm not thirteen anymore.

Linda, The Sculpture

Past and future
mesh
in the tv camera's eye,
me, ten years ago,
her, ten years later.
Whose side am I on?

I see the moment
she contains,
her peaceful pose.
I watch as her implanted hair,
freshly washed,
is shaped into curls.

I want to touch her hand,
hold onto the moment she is,
but I cannot.
Long after I am scattered ashes,
she will exist,
here, in the temperature
controlled museum,
being touched up
and brought out on view,
periodically.

I whisper goodbye
to her unchanging,
lifelike form.
I whisper goodbye
to my thirty-year-old self,
captured in her forever.
It is a new decade now.

Resting on her white pedestal,
she is protected by
high tech alarms,
oblivious to gangfire
and health insurance reform.
There are no repressed memories
waking her at night.
She is cared-for and safe.

She holds the peace
I once created
while covered in
a wet silicone mold,
an hour of serene thoughts
as I drifted away from
the chemical smell.

I shut my eyes and remember,
I can do it again,
even if only for an hour a day.
I can go to the place she is,
and rest.

OPEN

The room is swarming
with moths.
She says there's no point
trying to keep them
out, there's a hole
in the screen.
The windows are flung
open — hungry frogs
gulping moths.

I can't relax.

A cloud flutters
overhead
around the ceiling
light bulb, annoying
as bees.

How can she stand it?

Outside, inside
it's all the same, she says.
But outside, there are no
walls, no ceilings, no bulbs.
They disperse rather
than collect.
Still, they're better than mosquitoes.

Perfect Afternoon

Above
a curved roof of woven branches
triangles of light
enter
draw a patchwork quilt
below

Tucked under
the comfort of
shadows weight
slivers of crystal blue
peek in

Time stops

The deep perfume
of summer bliss
inhaled

STREAM, ST. LOUIS LAKE TRAIL

Glistening white sheets
splash bubbles
into the air
like clear, round ships
tossed over black rocks
the endless thrust
of life

THE WOODPECKER ARRIVES

His beak drums
against the metal chimney,
my annual notice
of spring.
When I hear the
woodpecker's drill,
I know the green lips
of tulip shoots will
soon push through their
blanket of dried leaves and
curl up out of their beds.
I will pack away
my winter wools,
spend more time
outside than in,
listening to my
winged reminder
that it is time
again
to begin.

I am in the Water Poem

The turquoise blue womb
fills me with peace,
washes out the ache inside.

Nikka scoots like a duckling
in her yellow tube,
wearing the all-teeth-showing, chin-out grin
that comes naturally to
two-year-olds.

Mom and Dad sit poolside,
bottles of Tanqueray and tonic
on the table, a big chunk missing
from the fresh lemon.

Nikka fills the barrel of her soaker,
squirts her Dad.
He retaliates with a full stream
spray from a larger gun.

I float on my back,
watch the moving, gray clouds
through pine branch lace.

I am in the water poem.
The words, my strokes, my breath,
a melodic rhythm.

Floating in the turquoise blue womb,
the sun filters through a break
in the clouds.
I'm not ready to be born.

How Long Can I Stay Here?

Standing in a patch of wildflowers
is a happy place
between the pussy willows
and stunted pines.
The tall bistort looks like
a turbanned ballerina
balancing on one foot.
The fluffy pink petals
of a paintbrush
are upside down petticoats
worn by green ladies
corralled by the perky
trunks of elephantella.

Yes, standing here
is a happy place,
enveloped by the sound
of the urgent river,
and I wonder,
how long
can I stay here?

WISHES

In my first wish
I am Poet Laureate.
Every morning I go to a
different school. The
students look up at me
with eager eyes,
sharpened pencils
and blank pages ready.
In the afternoons,
I walk,
my mind a sailboat
on a glassy sea.

In my second wish
my cabin is built.
Its golden logs reflect the
sun as it sets above Mt. Elbert.
I sit on the deck after dark
listening to the chatter of coyotes.
On the wood stove, a
kettle spouts steam.
At sleep,
silence encases me.
I awaken to a view, and
a grateful sigh,
greeted by my grove of aspens,
with its carpet of lupine,
aster and paintbrush.

In my third wish
I have a bowl that conjures up
whatever food I am craving.
Sometimes it's triple-death-chocolate ice cream,
but other times it's a greek salad—one
can have too much of a good thing.
I wouldn't want my wishes bringing
me misery, predictable or
otherwise. So, there you have it.
Squandered or fruitful, who can say?
There's no genie doling them out,
just me, imagining them first.

SEPTEMBER 11, 2001

Yesterday's frustrations recede
as news of crashing
hijacked planes
explode into my kitchen.
I watch as one of New York's
tallest towers crumbles,
trapping thousands in a massive
tomb of debris,
unable to erase the image
of people jumping
from the building.

The second tower succumbs.

Just two days ago
at 12,000 feet
wind floated across Gibson Lake,
mountains coated with fresh snow
dazzled against the cobalt sky,
marmots fattened for impending hibernation
sunned themselves on boulders
like vacationers at the beach.

Now peace seems so far away,
the world unsafe
as my thoughts scurry
like frightened mice
for a shelter
that doesn't exist.

Winter Morning

White gloved branches
glow in early morning's
gray pink light

WITHOUT INTRODUCTION

Standing near the lone, blue canoe
I notice the mosaic of pebbles
pounded into the dirt,
then the trash scattered like leaves,
the inevitable work of a raccoon.

I remember being awakened:

the unusual scraping sound
on the bark of my backyard maple.
Turning on the spotlight,
I am suddenly the intruder,
with the same awe as when I see
a marmot stand on its hind legs,
or an elk lope down the ridge,
or a moose cross the road.

I stare into the halloween mask
of your raccoon face.
We are both creatures,
beyond introduction,
simply alive.

Sometimes I feel as though
I am still looking out that window,
still startled,
surprised to be in the moment
we call life.

Outdoor Orchestra

A burst of wind across the valley
lifts cone-tipped branches
in a gentle bounce.
In the distance, the revved engine
of a motorcycle is
quickly masked by a
louder blast of wind.
At my feet, a carpet of
dry red needles, broken twigs
and fallen cones.
I sit still,
listening to the music.

Vendor

Mr. Sutera drove a cream-colored
station wagon.
In the back, round provolones hung on
ropes next to long salamis,
like the bodies of headless dolls.

When he got home, he filled
the cast iron tub with hot water,
scrubbed with Octagon soap,
boiled hot dogs for dinner,
opened a can of sauerkraut.

Rusted Key

Was it to an iron gate
to keep cattle from wandering?
Or was it to the door of this roofless cabin,
its logs sagging from too many winters,
abandoned decades ago by an unshaven miner,
a man with stale breath
and black lines deep in his hands
like veins of ore in rock,
the dream of yellow gold
rising like the sun each morning
in his determined heart.

What You Have Become

dense pine forest
undulates in wind
beneath harebell blue sky

no longer separate
not a thing to be chopped
or burnt for warmth
a part of the landscape

what you have become

INSIDE

caught on spinning planet
in brief cocoon
of connection
wings woven together
tucked away from
chill of outer world
safe
inside

Current Creek

Lime green shoots
rise up,
flags of summer thaw.
The water flings
bubbles onto
my legs. I am in
a small dry patch
surrounded by
snow, grateful to
whoever invented
the snowshoes that keep
me from sinking deep.
Everything is
melting, filling
the streams that
flow into rivers.
The movement of life
forward, forward
neverending.

North Carolina Hillbilly

When I think of you
I remember the doggy wallet
you gave me when I was itchy
from measles,
the blue of your eyes.

When I think of you
I see craters on the moon
close enough to touch through
the lens of your telescope,
stars you charted
with colored thumb tacks,
hanging in the basement.

I think of rocks you polished,
amethysts and tiger eyes made into necklaces,
the fine drafting instruments held
in narrow black cases lined with green velvet,
your grey metal tool box.

I hear the sounds of your shortwave
radio bringing faraway countries
into our house,
the hillbilly tunes you sang
while strumming your guitar.

I think of the old plough,
the garden rows you made,
corn growing tall in the summer's heat,
fireflies flickering above as we sat
on the porch, the chant of cicadas
harmonizing in the trees.

Now I hear the trickle of the brook.
It flows into earth,
returns to the deepest of all rivers,
the river that never ends.
I think about love,
how it, too, never ends,
about the only man
I'll ever call, "Dad."

Summer of Fires

I awaken to a peculiar orange
glow casting its light on the wall.
Forest fire smoke is blowing our way.
Driving into the mountains,
columns rise like twirling ghosts
above the ridge.

On the trail to Arapaho Lakes
the petals of the columbines
are the deepest purple I've ever seen.
The crimson caps of King's Crown
decorate the sides of the flowing creek.

We dip our feet in the
icy water of the lake. Wade in up to our
knees until we feel numb.
Resting on the shore, I feel the tickle
of flies exploring my legs.
Birds trill, a waterfall descends, a jet passes
overhead. I see the remnants of ski tracks
in a snow field at the back of the cirque.

Though a haze of smoke
obscures the usual crisp view,
close up,
the beauty remains.

Leonid Meteor Shower

Out of the tent at 3:00 a.m.
looking up at the bounty
only visible at 10,000 feet.
Stars fly across the sky,
a rush of
silent fireworks,
their heads bright spots of fire,
their tails fuzzy streamers.
I can't turn my head fast enough.
I count 569 in ninety minutes.

Back in my bag,
I drift into comet dreams,
emerge hours later to
a light snow falling.

Sipping coffee hot off the Coleman stove
I watch the sun lift the mist
from the neighboring peaks.

Sitting amongst leaf-stripped aspen
I dip my wash cloth into water,
press it against my face,
as a squirrel talks to me
from a nearby pine.

The day will come
when a log cabin is built here,
a cabin I have long imagined.
I see it now as clearly as last night's
shooting stars, flying across the sky,
as promised.

High Cholesterol Blues

I dream of pancakes
piled on my plate
layered with butter,
maple syrup flowing
across them like a
spring stream,
but instead
I eat oatmeal.
I dream of creamy milkshakes
so thick they
have to be eaten
with a spoon,
but instead
I eat an apple.
I am surrounded by reduced-fat this
and fat-free that.
The doctor says I need
a prescription,
but I am as determined
as a bull in a pen.
I run, I buy a low-fat cookbook.
I am the model of discipline.
I recall the days of
quiche lorraine, pizza
and ice cream
as if they were as distant
as my youth.
I boldly flaunt
my banner,
"Less than 20 grams of fat per day"
and I know that I will
taste victory
even if it isn't sweet.

To Be Deaf

I sit in the puffy recliner chair in the corner
staring at nothing.
My cat is at my feet, purring.
Through the open window, I hear the chirp
of crickets, the drip of my neighbor's fountains
and the light stirring of leaves.
I think about what it would be like to be deaf.
What is it like to not hear thunder
or the sound of a fast flowing mountain stream
cascading over rocks?
Is it like being trapped in a padded cell?
Is there some kind of white noise
generated from within?
The thought startles me like a scream.

Seed of Joy

She knew it was in there,
though she hadn't touched it.
But she had felt it rise up
inside her like a snake
trained to dance,
his head above the ground at last,
tongue clicking,
scales gleaming like polished rocks,
the rattle of his voice
bringing silence to the crowd.
It was the kind of lifting up
she knew was possible,
knew that someday
she would have.

Snatches of Space

Bare branches
cut shapes
in the blue sky,
days I remember:
small snatches
of space,
hours of clear comfort.

What remains?
The solid trunk of the tree,
the contrast of its old limbs
with new growth.
The spring that will
come again
bringing buds for squirrels
to nibble.
The memories
distant, brittle,
like fragile leaves,
crumbling.

Backwards

In the backwards universe
our clothes choose us.
They float off closet hangers,
unzip and pull themselves
over our heads.
Colors always match.

Cars are free agents
roaming the streets.
With a honk of a horn
they stop to pick us up.
A click of the windshield wipers
makes them pull over
to let us out.

In the backwards universe
food grows inside our cupboards,
stays fresh and is always ripe for picking.
There is no packaging or waste.

Rivers flow straight up like fountains,
rainbows splatter the sidewalks,
traffic lights are varying shades of purple
and no one stops.

Mosquitoes flutter like butterflies,
singing the chords of a harp,
metallic strips hang on patios
to attract them.

Everyone wants to cry, not laugh.
Prescriptions are sold
to make you introspective.
People are content to grow old.
When the moon is full
it makes a black hole in a white sky.

Our journals are already written.
We read them,
go to bed,
then turn on the lights.

FUNERAL

I toss the peach petaled rose
into the hole
the hole
that holds
your dead body

Everyone else
has returned
to their cars
to escape
the downpour

I stand in the rain
stare at the delicate
petals that landed
on top of your
casket
I cannot move
I cannot say goodbye
Forever is too long
to stay inside my heart

WHEN SHE SMILES
    for Chloe and Carl

When she smiles,
the bare branches
of aspen fan
like peacock feathers
to greet her.

Snow collects
in the cirques,
draws outlines of
ridges, turns
rocks into puffs
of white cream.

When she smiles,
the moon sheds
its haze,
constellations emerge
clear as Castle Creek.

Smoke from chimneys
of log cabins
curl into scripts,
spelling warm words.

Inside she sits,
her chocolate brown eyes
glowing in the light
of the hearth,
her hand in his,
the door of love
opened,

calling them down
its path.

A path that will
always be brightened
when she smiles.

BITTER

As cold as a glacier,
harder than marble,
that's the way you are.
Feelings roll away from you
like debris in an avalanche,
collect in a pile
far beneath
your peak of superiority.
They linger like frost
on a bitter morning
refusing to melt.

Laid Off

What is there about a parking lot
where you lift a plastic window, feed
in your five dollar bill, place the
receipt on your dash,
or the couple you pass
walking on the street each day
always holding hands,
or the way you put your sunglasses
back in their case while
you wait for the elevator?

What is there about a chair with
a taped-on pillow, a cushy bumper in
front of the keyboard, a password,
that makes you feel
like you belong,
like you are part of the world?

And then, in one sentence,
it is gone.

For Chuck on his 80th Birthday

You just missed a golden opportunity to keep your mouth
   shut!
Harvard researchers say the road to Hell is paved with good
   intentions.

The Duke of Cumberland can't get a word in edgewise.
Lord Cesspool had the good taste to die.

Hey, Armbruster, you never listen to me.
You go on about your rat killing.

My wife, Rebecca Jeanne, and things too fierce to mention.
Patience Pudding with Wait-and-See Sauce.

Lucky Pierre! Always in ze middle.
And this is the chapel at Pomfret.

Head for the water.
The sun's over the yardarm.

Julia

Out of twenty-three
only you
have it
missing.
When
did it
disappear?
Days, weeks,
months
after birth?
Once I thought
I saw a
glimpse
when you
skipped
into the room
after show
and tell,
but usually
you just sit
against the
chainlink fence,
face hidden
by hair,
quiet as a
floating feather,
the girl
without light
in her eyes.

Aunt Lala

There was only one.
Who else would knit
slipper socks to warm my feet?
Who else would crochet me
a black shawl whose pattern
was written in italian?
Who else would crochet the
matching string bikinis
in white and beige
that I wore in college?

There was only one aunt
I visited on every trip east.
We'd sit at the kitchen table
sipping tea. From a drawer
in her dining room hutch,
a box of Perugina "Baci's"
would emerge.

How can I describe her voice,
a raspy instrument?
Or her petite frame,
home to such a feisty spirit?

She is not gone.

I remember getting on a plane,
a plastic container of her
homemade pesto in my bag.
Later, the perfect blend
of fragrant basil and olive oil
rose from fresh pasta
in my kitchen.

I picture her house,
the absence of her being.

Refractions of our time
together bounce across
the room like rainbows from
a crystal hanging
in a window,
and I am grateful.

Lost

Holding the single blue mitten,
it struck me when she said,
"It's so small,"
as if I'd been forcing him
to wear something
long outgrown.

Why these tears?
We got our money's worth,
many season's of use.

Is it the size of
the one left,
showing how much
he's grown?

Or is it the window
I know I will stand at
after the door
has shut behind him,
in a future
made less distant
by a lost, blue mitten?

Can You See?

I wonder what it's like to be
the bird high up in the pine tree,
huge puffs of snow piled on its branches?

I wonder what it's like to be
the caerulean damsel fish swimming
through coral reefs, with anemones
undulating all around you?

I wonder what it is like
where you are now
far away from your favorite
chair and short wave radio,
stock car races and weekly
phone calls, fights over cigarettes?

What is this place you have
entered? Who was there to
greet you? Did you know
I was there at your side
those nine long visits,
singing and holding your hand,
while you lay there helpless,
finally in a place where you
could receive affection
without pushing it away?

Can you look back now
and see the purity of love
as pure as this snow at my feet?
Can you drift around like air,
crossing between this world
and the next, can you see
my tears?

PRISON

Inside
no light
no trees
no blue sky
Why can't I break free
from the prison of myself?
Stuck in the gray concrete
of old belief
needing to bend the bars
escape into a brighter world.

Hiking Questions in Canyonlands

Is it some geological joke
that these rocks look like the
lopsided crowns of flopped muffins?

Were those hanging slices of toast
accidentally dropped from heaven's plate?

Maybe I've traveled further than I realized in this
space ship rock, peering out of its round windows,
or emerged from that submarine now docked above ground.

However I got here,
I'm hooked on this fractured, eroded sandstone.
I'd like to live in this city of spires,
with its on-site architects, wind and water,
share habitat with pale-skinned lizards
and flapping ravens,
carve a piece of my own space
in this silence.

The Visitor

He walks in
pace purposeful
brisk
as if he's heading
for a subway
due to arrive.

He slaps down his leather bag
on the desk,
whaap.
Takes out what looks like an
electric screwdriver,
pulls out a metal extension,
click.

This is a creative writing class.
He says, "Don't mind me."
But we do mind.
We want to know,
who is he?
What is he doing?
What is that sharp metal projection?

Whirr
He begins swinging a black device.
As our mouths form "o's"
in our turned heads
he informs us,
"I'm just measuring the room temperature
and humidity."

I want to say,
"Since you walked in,
both went up."

EYE TO EYE

When you didn't
arrive
I thought maybe
you forgot or
were lost or
maybe you were
like the deer
I saw in the woods.

I thought he was speaking
to me with those dark,
bulging eyes,
the way he slowly lifted
a thin leg
up onto a rock,
moved closer,
a current running
between us.
We stood like that
plugged in
eye to eye.
Then, a voice.

Back at trailhead
a bow hunter
stopped me,
asked if I'd
seen any deer.

I imagined you safe
in the thicket of bushes,
nibbling autumn grass,
wise to not get
too close.

EDDY

I feel like a boat heading
upstream.
Is there a wing to lift me up,
place me in a new spot
where I flow along
as peacefully as an alpine
stream bordered by the
hot pink of Parry's Primrose,
immersed in the music
of trickling water,
the source of life,
instead of where I am now,
bumping against boulders,
caught in a circular eddy,
going nowhere.

The Details

He notices right off
that the sunglasses
around my neck
are ceramic
and not functional,
then my watch
whose hands are tubes of paint
and that there are no numbers,
just three blobs of color.
Then he asks about my bracelet.
what it's made of—
aluminum I say—
He says, "Everything you've
got on is unique."
Kids always notice these things.

Our attention comes back
to the fact that we are in
the library on a hot afternoon.
This is homework club.
I am helping three sixth grade boys with math,
specifically, theoretical probability.
We have a list of sandwiches, vegetables and cookies.
We determine that twelve combinations are possible,
that ten of those contain at least one
of "Joelyn's three favorite items."

I suck on the straw jammed into
my Starbuck's iced mocha.
I ask to be pardoned for slurping.
I like to get the very last drop.
The boys are non-chalant, after all,
I know how obsessed they are at that age
with burping and farting, I live with

a sixth grader.
Later at home, I help my son with
the very same homework.
It's fun being one step ahead.

The sun slowly travels over my roof,
shifting its rays from the dining room
window to the bedroom.

I assemble ingredients for an enchilada bake:
refried beans, cheddar cheese, green chilis,
salsa verde and chopped tomatoes
layered over corn tortillas.

With the clock change, there's still enough light
on the terrace after dinner to read. These first
warm days of spring are sweet as homegrown corn.

I sink back into the patio chair,
look up at the branches
just beginning to dress in buds.
My cat's head swivels every time
a bird moves through the air.

I stretch my legs over to my son's chair,
rest my feet alongside him. He responds with
his own feet propped against my legs.
His feet are almost as long as mine.
Hard to remember that just twelve years ago,
I sat out here on an unseasonably warm winter day,
with him bundled in a blanket, nursing him.

Hard to imagine what it must be like in Baghdad
amidst bombed out rubble, the unrelenting thud
of fired artillery in the air, the curtains of smoke,
clouding the details
of daily life.

What a Poem Can Be

Walk with me
under a purple-green sky
where a tornado sweeps you up
like a magic carpet and
takes you where you want to be.

A poem can be
any color of the rainbow—
the shape of a shell,
something you see
or feel,
a combination of words
that fit like a puzzle.

You are the creator.
You draw the stars
that shine,
lighting up the heavens
the way you see it
at 10,000 feet.

Walk with me
in the world of words,
where pens are the soldiers
succumbing to the bidding
of our dancing imaginations.

Let the words
lead you
like the bars
of a song
you sing.
Our voices
will fill
the room.

INDEX OF ILLUSTRATIONS BY JOHN BOAK

Fourth of July	6
St. Louis Lake	10
South Crestone Lake	14
Huron Peak	18
Ohman Lake	24
Whale Creek	28
Murray Creek	32
Arapaho Pass	38
King, Betty & Bob	50
Elephant Canyon	52
Dry Gulch	56
Mt. Democrat	60

ABOUT THE AUTHOR

Comet Dreams is Linda Keller's fifth book of poetry. Her other books include *Deep in the Wilderness, You Can Stop Longing,* and the limited edition chapbooks, *Making Up the Way* and *Here I am.* She teaches poetry in area schools. A passionate hiker, she has lived in Colorado since 1977.

ABOUT THE ARTIST

John Boak received his B.A. in Fine Art from Yale University in 1970. The illustrations in this book were made from the color drawings he makes while hiking with Linda and their son, Canyon, in the mountains. In addition to oil paintings of these landscapes, he also makes painted abstract wall sculptures that incorporate symbols he has drawn throughout his career.